**W9-AMX-402**

DATE DUE		
SEP 23 '89	DEC 15 '94	FEB 6 1999
OCT 10 '89	JUL 12 '95	
APR 5 '90	DEC 5 '95	
APR 27 '90		
MAY 11 '90	_Jennifer Von_	
OCT 12 '90	MAY 8 '96	
JUN 29 '91	MAY 17 '96	
APR 2 '92	JUN 16 '96	
NOV 19 '93	MAR 6 '97	
MAR 4 '94	MAR 3 '98	
MAY 5 '94	MAR 17 '98	

GIANT PANDA

CONTENTS

© Aladdin Books Ltd 1989

Designed and produced by
Aladdin Books Ltd
70 Old Compton Street
London W1

First published in the
United States in 1989 by
Gloucester Press
387 Park Avenue South
New York, NY 10016

Printed in Belgium

Design Rob Hillier
Editor Denny Robson
Researcher Cecilia Weston-Baker
Illustrator Ron Hayward Associates

ISBN 0-531-17140-X

Library of Congress Catalog
Card Number: 88-83104

PROJECT WILDLIFE

GIANT PANDA

Michael Bright

Gloucester Press
New York : London : Toronto : Sydney

◁ This is the symbol of the World
Wildlife Fund (WWF).

▽ A Giant Panda in its mountain
forest home in winter.

The Giant Panda is in danger. The cuddly-looking, black-and-white animal with the clownish face is the symbol of the World Wildlife Fund (WWF) and the symbol of wildlife protection everywhere. But despite world concern and nearly a decade of international conservation work to try to save the Giant Panda, the animal is still on the brink of extinction.

The Giant Panda was known as the *bei-shung*, or white bear, to the ancient Chinese. But even those who lived in panda country rarely saw one. Western scientists were unaware that it existed until the French priest, Père David, discovered it on one of his expeditions to China in 1869. Its rarity and its unusual coat made it a desirable target for hunters.

Today pandas are still trapped, illegally, for their skins. More importantly, the wild places in which they live are being destroyed. There are now fewer than 1,000 Giant Pandas surviving in the wild and their numbers are still dwindling.

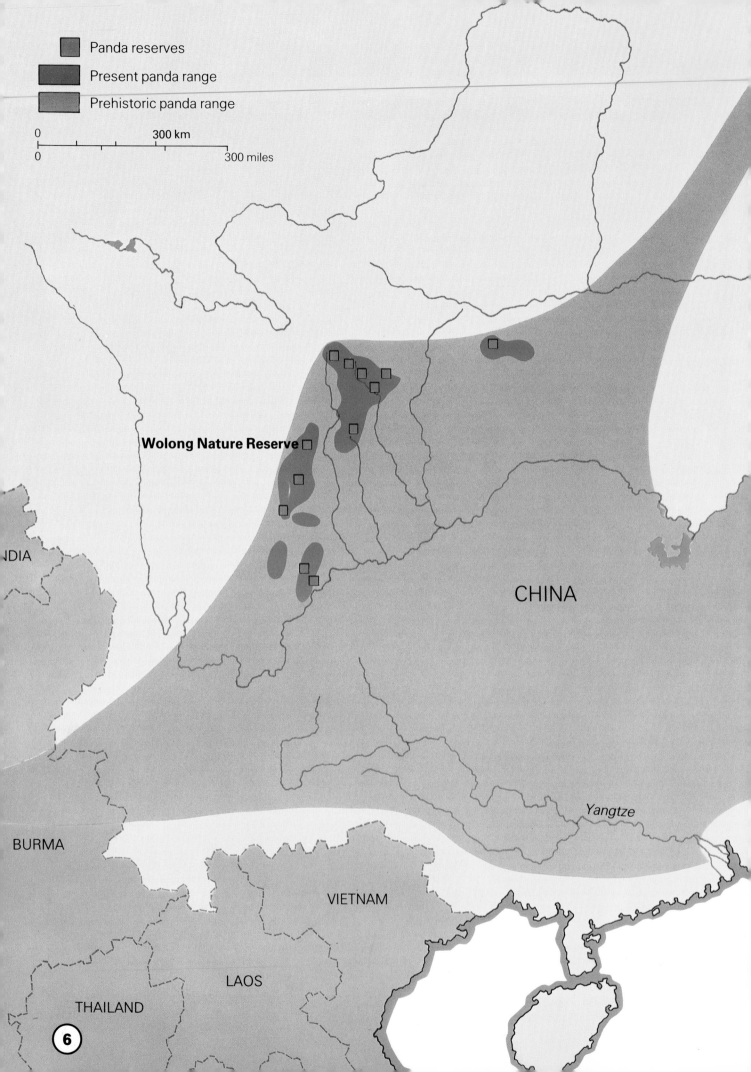

Panda reserves

Present panda range

Prehistoric panda range

0   300 km

0   300 miles

Wolong Nature Reserve

INDIA

CHINA

Yangtze

BURMA

VIETNAM

LAOS

THAILAND

6

Panda distribution

Giant Pandas live in the mountainous regions of the Sichuan, Gansu and Shaanxi provinces in China. Fossils of Giant Pandas show that they were once widely distributed throughout China and in Burma. But today they only exist in small scattered populations, mostly in the high mountains and deep ravines of Sichuan province. Human activities, like farming, have pushed them up to the higher wooded slopes of mountains. Their range now covers a total area of only 6,500 square kilometers (2,500 square miles) – a very small area compared to their past range. Pandas might also exist in isolated populations in the remote areas of Tibet.

The Giant Panda's preferred habitat – the place where it lives – is cold, damp, thick bamboo forests. These are sandwiched between farmland on the lower slopes and the dense rhododendron forests higher up. The panda belt is between 1,500 and 4,000 meters (4,900-13,000 ft) high. Pandas are very elusive animals. They hide in the remaining bamboo forests avoiding people and therefore they are rarely seen.

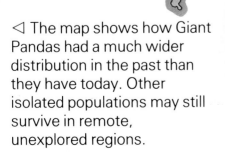

◁ The map shows how Giant Pandas had a much wider distribution in the past than they have today. Other isolated populations may still survive in remote, unexplored regions.

△ This is Giant Panda country in Wolong, China.

The panda skin trade

After Père David's discovery, Giant Pandas became targets for the big game hunters. But despite the demand for skins (particularly by the world's museums) very few were killed. Pandas were able to hide in their thick, dense forests. In 1962 the export of panda skins was banned. But there is still a demand for the bold black and white skins to make ornamental rugs. A new trade has developed. Today pandas are trapped and often strangled in wire snares by poachers. In the Wolong Reserve, there were 145 pandas in 1974. In 1986 there were only 72. Many had been killed by poachers.

"Dear Sirs, We are pleased to learn that you appreciate and collect some valued things. We should like to inform you that we get specimens of panda fur from Hong Kong. If you are interested in purchasing it, please don't hesitate to write to us."

Letter from the Ruey Pin Trading Company to Birmingham Museum, UK, 1983.

△ This is Chi-Chi who lived in Peking, Moscow, Frankfurt, Copenhagen and London. She died in 1972 and her body is now on display in the British Museum, London.

The scarcity of Giant Pandas today means that their skins are very valuable. Some people think it is chic to own the skins of rare animals and are prepared to pay vast sums of money. Panda skins are smuggled out of China to traders in Hong Kong. They are then re-exported for sale in Japan and Taiwan. Rewards are high, both for the Chinese peasants who risk arrest and imprisonment, and the Japanese dealers who may be caught by customs officials. Recently a pair of panda skins was sold for $200,000. Tempted by these large sums of money, dealers have even offered live animals to private zoos.

▽ This shopkeeper displays many different types of furs for sale. It is unlikely that he would openly show a panda skin because he would be arrested. Some shops in Thailand, Singapore and Hong Kong have "back rooms" in which the illegally acquired furs are kept. Some dealers claim they can supply panda skins on demand.

Habitat destruction

China has a population of about one billion people – the largest population in the world. All these people need space in which to live and land on which to grow food. As a result, as the Chinese population continues to expand, the panda's previously safe home high in the mountains is slowly being destroyed. Farmers are clearing undergrowth further and further up the mountains to plant their crops. Pandas are unable to make their seasonal migrations up and down the mountains. They are hemmed in by mountains above and fields below. They have to live on a narrow band of mountain slope.

Throughout the panda's range, the mountain forests are being cut down. In Sichuan alone, trees are felled at a rate of one percent a year. In one of the largest Giant Panda reserves at Wolong, 14 sq km (5.4 sq miles) of forest have been hacked down by peasants during the last decade. The authorities appear to be powerless to stop the destruction. In fact, the rate of felling and clearing is increasing. Conservationists believe that it is the destruction of the panda's living space that will eventually kill off the panda in the wild. The Giant Panda will simply have nowhere to live.

◁ This village and its vegetable plots (top) are on the lower slopes in the mountains of Sichuan Province. Vast areas of land have been cleared of their trees (left) to supply much needed wood and to make way for farming.

The Giant Panda is not the only form of wildlife that is threatened by the destruction of the mountain forests. There are also 300 different kinds of birds and mammals living among 4,000 known species of wild plants like rhododendrons, lilies and roses. All of these are losing ground as civilization encroaches on the wilderness.

The bamboo problem

The invasion of Giant Panda country by humans, the short-term problem of poaching, and the long-term problem of habitat destruction are not the only threats to the panda's survival. Nature itself has delivered a cruel blow. Giant Pandas feed mainly on the leaves and stems of bamboo. Once every 15 to 120 years, depending on the species of bamboo, huge sections of the bamboo forest burst into flower at the same time. Seeds are set and then all the bamboo plants die back. With the disappearance of the bamboo, the pandas are deprived of their main supply of food. This can be disastrous for the pandas.

The Giant Panda prefers two types of bamboo above the 700 others — the arrow and the umbrella bamboos. Arrow bamboo stands 1 to 2m (3-6 ft) tall and is found on the lower slopes. Logging and farming have removed umbrella bamboo, so when arrow bamboo flowers the pandas have nothing to eat.

▽ The scientist below is weighing bamboo stems. He is finding out how much food pandas need to eat to stay alive and well.

▷ The panda on the right is sitting in the typical panda eating position. It is eating bamboo plants that have not yet died back.

At one time, pandas could avoid going hungry by migrating to another part of the forest where another species of bamboo was not flowering. But today the forests have been cut down. Only isolated patches are left. And the pandas can no longer travel safely across their former habitat. Without the precious bamboo, they die. During the past decade, several reserves have had bamboo "die-back." In the mid 1970s most of the arrow bamboo in the Wolong Reserve flowered at the same time. At the end of 1987 when the crisis had passed, a total of 62 Giant Pandas had been found dead from starvation.

The fight against poaching

△ In such beautiful but remote countryside, the authorities find it difficult to keep track of poachers.

To help reduce poaching, there is now a system of rewards for looking after pandas and also an education program. Local farmers learn to respect pandas. Recently a farmer found a panda asleep in his sheep pen. He was careful not to disturb it. But later he found it had run off with his lunch!

◁ Pandas may climb and hide in trees to avoid predators.

In China, the Giant Panda is a valuable and treasured animal. Chinese authorities are doing all they can to save it from extinction. Unfortunately, however, anti-poaching patrols are not common – resources are needed elsewhere. But the law is strict. Since 1987, poachers can be sentenced to death if they kill a panda. Some gangs have already received life imprisonment. During 1987, 133 poachers were arrested. Recently, two Chinese seamen caught with panda skins were given suspended jail sentences and fined a total of $11,000. Life sentences are now given.

But very few of the poachers and smugglers are caught, and there are plenty more to take the place of those who are. The effect of poaching on the declining panda population is serious. Female pandas reproduce slowly. They mature after five years and only rear one cub every two to three years. Poaching could mean that death rates could exceed birth rates. If this happened, wild pandas would be wiped out.

Helping pandas in the wild

◁ Research work in the cold and damp bamboo forests is not comfortable. In winter the air temperature can be well below zero and ice can form on the inside of the tent wall. Fog can cover the forest.

Researchers can monitor a panda's position and movements during the day and night by using radio tracking. A slow pulsing signal indicates an animal at rest whereas a fast signal shows that the animal is active, either feeding or moving. The radio signals are checked every 15 minutes, for twenty-four hours a day.

In order to help the Giant Panda to survive, we need to know more about the way it lives. In 1979 China, with the support and encouragement of the organization, World Wildlife Fund (WWF), launched the "Save the Panda" project. Much of the conservation effort in recent years has gone towards observing pandas in the wild. But this is not easy. Pandas are shy animals and they avoid people. It is also difficult to travel through panda country without being detected. Pandas can hear the noisy footsteps of an approaching observer and move away. Many researchers have spent months in the bamboo forests without ever seeing a panda.

Today some pandas are caught, put to sleep, and fitted with radio collars that transmit a "bleep." When the panda wakes up and is released back into the wild, scientists with portable receivers can follow it from a distance and monitor its daily routine. The pandas very quickly get used to wearing the collars and behave quite normally.

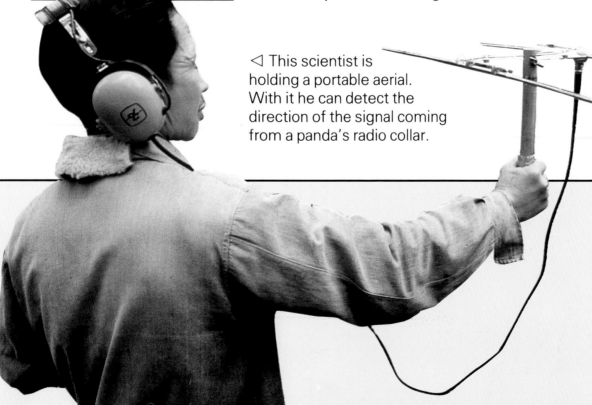

◁ This scientist is holding a portable aerial. With it he can detect the direction of the signal coming from a panda's radio collar.

More help for pandas

At times of great hardship for the Giant Pandas the Chinese authorities have stepped in to help them. During the last major period of bamboo flowering and die-back, hundreds of forest workers combed the remote hillsides searching for starving pandas. Some 25 were caught and moved to other areas where the bamboo was not flowering. Another 47 were taken into captivity, but 12 soon died. In some areas, the peasants fed the hungry pandas from their own meager food supplies. Some pandas broke into houses and stole food.

▽ The panda is lured into the trap (below) by baiting it with rotting sheep heads. It is transferred to a lightweight carrying cage (below right and overleaf). Many pandas, don't trust the log traps and have to be caught with foot snares. These are not the bone-breaking traps used by poachers, but safe, lightweight traps. All the traps are checked twice each day.

In some reserves, additional food supplies were carried in by 20 WWF pick-up trucks to help a few individuals to survive. Although bamboo is their main food, Giant Pandas will accept other foods. They like sugarcane, apples, meat and bones. In one village in Sichuan province a starving panda was presented with a whole roast sheep.

Another visited a research camp where it took to eating porridge. One farmer found a starving panda which had fallen over a cliff. He carried it on his tractor to the nearest town, 50 miles away, and received a reward.

During the bamboo crisis, rescue money came from all over the world. It included $13,000 from "Pennies for Pandas" collected by schoolchildren in the United States. A Japanese television company paid $100,000 to film the rescue. The whole rescue operation cost nearly $2 million.

△ A captured panda is moved to the research center.

△ The Wolong Research and Conservation Center.

The Wolong Reserve

There are twelve panda reserves in China. Ten are in Sichuan province and the largest is Wolong — 494,000 acres of mountain forest, 3,700 meters (12,000 ft) above sea level in the Qionglai Mountains. It is home to 3,000 Quaing people who farm the slopes, and home to one eighth of the world's pandas. At Wolong there is the Research Center for the Protection of the Giant Panda and its Ecosystem, jointly funded by the WWF and the Chinese government. The center observes and counts the pandas in the reserve, and it also has a captive breeding farm that includes a veterinary hospital and nursery.

The center also has a project studying panda food. Scientists are searching for substitutes for the arrow and umbrella bamboos which pandas like best. They are planting different species and watching to see which ones the pandas prefer. Recently, they discovered that pandas like rye grass. This might help feed pandas when the bamboo is flowering.

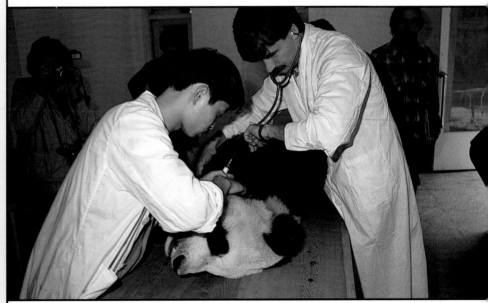

△ Wolong veterinarians treating a panda.

Captive breeding may be a way to save the Giant Panda.

Pandas in zoos

Because of their cuddly, teddy-bear appearance and playful nature, Giant Pandas have been very popular in zoos. But they are very difficult to keep in captivity. Many, including new-born cubs, have died.

There are less than 100 pandas in captivity in China and another 16 in six zoos around the world. It was once thought that it was important to take the animals and breed them in captivity, and later release them back into the wild. But today this thinking is being questioned. Pandas in zoos are poor at breeding. In China, only two or three cubs are born each year, usually the result of artificial insemination (the female conceives and bears young without having to mate). In zoos in other countries the situation is worse.

The problem is complex – pandas only come into heat for a few days each year, male pandas are often reluctant to mate, and cubs do not survive well in captivity. In the wild Giant Pandas breed without trouble. It seems we cannot create the right conditions in zoos. But there has been some success. Mexico City Zoo has had four cubs since 1981 and in China's Chengdu Zoo a panda named Mei-Mei recently gave birth to her sixth cub since 1980.

'Chia-Chia' London Zoo to Washington

British airways cargo
We'll take more care.

British airways cargo pampers Pandas

△ Pandas are sometimes moved to different zoos.

It is hoped they will mate, but so far efforts have failed.

The panda's future

The Giant Panda has always been important to China. In AD 685, the Emperor of China gave panda skins and live pandas to Japan. China used to give pandas as gifts to friendly nations. Today there is a "rent-a-panda" policy which allows animals to be loaned to foreign zoos. The money raised is put into panda conservation. Some people are worried that because money is involved, this program may mean that more animals are caught and put in zoos.

An enormous amount of money and effort has gone into saving the Giant Panda. So far it has failed to stop the decline in their numbers. The animal's future is in the hands of one country, and sadly its future looks bleak. The panda's living space is disappearing, pandas are being killed by poachers, and many pandas are being taken from the wild and placed into expensive cages. Soon the only Giant Pandas left will be seen behind bars.

▷ Unless things change, the future for this panda and her cub looks bleak.

"The situation of the Giant Panda illustrates virtually all the problems confronting the world of living nature. All these problems derive from one basic source – the phenomenal success of one particular species – *Homo Sapiens*."

Prince Philip, President of the World Wildlife Fund

▽ Prince Philip, meets a panda cub in China. It is one of the few that has survived.

Panda fact file 1

The Giant Panda stands 70-80cm (27-31 in.) at the shoulder and weighs 100-150kg (220-330 lb). When upright on its hind legs it can measure 170cm (60 in.) from head to toe. Males tend to be about 10 percent larger than females. The Giant Panda's lifespan is not known, but we do know that captive pandas live to about 20 years old.

Panda markings

Giant Pandas are white, except for their ears, eye patches, muzzle, limbs and shoulders, which are black. The Chinese used to think of the Giant Panda as a white bear, *bei-shung*. The function of the bold black and white markings is not clear. At certain times of the day the animal is very conspicuous, but at others it tends to blend in with its background. It is thought that the markings may give some kind of camouflage in the bamboo forests at dawn and dusk, when shadows are long and pandas are most active. This form of camouflage is also particularly effective in winter. Against the snow, black rocks and trees, the panda becomes invisible.

The panda's range

Pandas are solitary animals. They each have a small home range covering up to 1,655 acres. The living space of females overlaps, except for a small corner in each female's range.

Several males may share the home range but they make sure to avoid meeting each other. Scent markings on rocks and tree trunks act as "keep out" signs. Males only meet other males when competing for the attentions of a female.

For most of the year, pandas stay in the higher mountain forests, but in spring some descend to lower slopes to feed on young bamboo shoots.

Daily life

Giant Pandas spend about 14 hours a day feeding and ten hours resting. They sleep for two to four hours at a time. The most active parts of the day are in the early morning and late afternoon, although they might forage at any time of the day or night. Sometimes they scrape trees with their claws. It is not clear why, but maybe it is another panda sign to say "keep out." When one panda meets another, for example when a female is ready to mate, they greet each other with grunts, yips and chirps.

Food and feeding

Food mainly consists of bamboo stems and leaves. The panda eats in a very human-like way. It sits on its haunches with a stem in its forepaws and brings the food up to its mouth. The bamboo is grasped in the teeth and the outer covering is stripped away. The center part is crushed by the huge cheek teeth into small pieces and swallowed.

The intestine is surprisingly short for an animal that eats tough plant food. Much of the leaves and stems pass right through undigested. The food is not very nutritious and the panda's digestive system is so inefficient that a panda must eat an enormous amount of food in order to gain enough nutrients to stay alive. It feeds for about a third of its waking life, chomping through about 18kg of arrow bamboo a day. In spring, some pandas eat the new shoots of umbrella bamboo on the lower slopes. They are mostly water and so a panda must eat 40kg every day.

Pandas are not exclusively vegetarian. They supplement their diet with meat and insects when available – rats in the bamboo stands, beetles, and sometimes leftovers from a leopard kill. In captivity they have been known to eat just about anything.

Pandas get water from bamboo, but sometimes they will drink. They scoop out a hollow next to a stream and when it is filled with water they drink as much as they can. They waddle away with swollen stomachs.

In some villages Giant Pandas are known as "iron bears." They have stolen cooking pots and eaten chunks out of the sides. Their strong teeth and jaws can chew up the metal which then passes straight through the stomach.

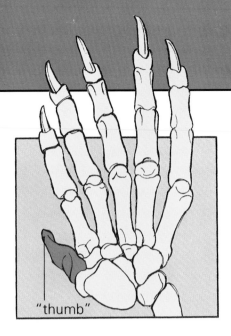

"thumb"

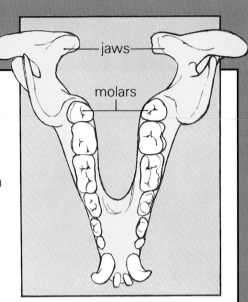

jaws

molars

Fingers and jaws

Pandas hold the bamboo stems in a special bony thumb-like projection or sixth claw (left) in the wrist of the forepaws.

The broad, flat molar teeth and the heavy jaws with powerful muscles (right) can strip and crush hard stems.

Courtship

Giant Pandas are mature and ready to mate when they are four to five years old. It is the only time they come together. A female may attract several males who compete for her attention.

Male pandas may fight for an hour or more. They charge together, again and again, without hurting each other. They roar and pant until, at some invisible signal, one gives up and goes away.

The mating period is from mid-March to early May, although each female is only receptive for about three to four days a year. Courtship involves the exchange of a series of calls.

Newborn cubs

The gestation period for the Giant Panda can vary between 97 to 163 days. In August or September, the female finds a maternity den, usually in the hollow base of a large fir tree. There she gives birth to two underdeveloped, pink, naked and blind cubs. Each cub is only 15cm (6in.) long and weighs 100-150g (3.5-5.3 oz).

Growing up

Although a female panda has twins, she cannot carry, hold and suckle two helpless babies. Usually one cub is ignored and dies. The other is fed 6-14 times per day for the first week of its life.

The panda cub's eyes open at one and a half to two months and the cub does not move about itself for about three months. It is weaned at six months. The mother is never far from the den. Youngsters are easy prey for leopards.

Many infant pandas die of unknown causes. Pandas, for example, suffer from serious roundworm infestations. Those that survive predators and diseases become independent of their mothers at the end of their first year.

About 50 million years ago, the bears, raccoons and pandas had a common ancestor. Between 30 and 50 million years ago the bears and the raccoons split away from each other. Not long afterward New World raccoons and Old World raccoons (red or Lesser Pandas) split. And then about 20 million years ago the Giant Pandas split away from the bears.

Raccoon

Nearest relative debate

There has been a great scientific debate about which animals are the Giant Panda's nearest relatives. Some say the Giant Panda is raccoon (top right) and therefore related to the Lesser Panda (bottom right). Others say it should be grouped with the bears (middle right). Researchers at the National Cancer Institute and the National Zoological Park in Washington DC used the very latest biology tests, revealing differences and similarities between animals. They concluded that the Giant Panda is, as any child can see, a black and white bear.

Its similarity to the red-haired Lesser Panda — tooth structure, skull shape and fur color pattern — is the result of the two animals adopting similar lifestyles in their Himalayan home.

Brown bear

Lesser Panda

Index

Photographic Credits:
Cover and page 13 (background): Ardea;
pages 4-5, 13, 14, 15, 16, 18, 19, 20 (both),
23, 25, 26, 27 (both), 29, 30 (both) and 31
(bottom): Rex Features; pages 7 and 10-11
(bottom): Planet Earth; pages 8, 10-11 (top),
12, 17, 22 and 28: Bruce Coleman; page 21:
World Wildlife Fund International; page 24:
Julian Calder; page 31 (both): Survival Anglia.

PRINTED IN BELGIUM BY
proost
INTERNATIONAL BOOK PRODUCTION